PLAZA

Independence Day

Willma Willis Gore

Reading Consultant:

Michael P. French, Ph.D.
Bowling Green State University

—Best Holiday Books—

Enslow Publishers, Inc.

44 Fadem Road	PO Box 38
Box 699	Aldershot
Springfield, NJ 07081	Hants GU12 6BP
USA	UK

> *To Audrey, Marilyn and Shirley*
> *With loving appreciation for constant*
> *support and encouragement.*

Library of Congress Cataloging-in-Publication Data

Gore, Willma Willis.
    Independence Day / Willma Willis Gore.
        p. cm. — (Best holiday books)
    Includes index.
    Summary: Describes the origins and past and present celebrations
of Independence Day.
    ISBN 0-89490-403-5
    1. Fourth of July—Juvenile literature. 2. Fourth of July
celebrations—Juvenile literature. [1. Fourth of July.]
I. Title. II. Series.
    E286.A12975 1993
   394.2'684'0973—dc20
                                   92-18946
                                       CIP
                                     AC

Printed in the United States of America

10 9 8 7 6 5 4 3

Illustration Credits:
Donald Lee Stovall, p. 43; Ed King, p. 16; Independence National Historical Park
Collection, pp. 9, 39; Mrs. Kevin Scheibel, p. 4; Library of Congress, p. 10; Myer
S. Bornstein, p. 41; National Archives, pp. 14, 23; Washington, D.C. Convention and
Visitors Association, p. 19; Willma Willis Gore, pp. 25, 28, 31, 32, 37.

Cover Illustration:
Charlott Nathan

Contents

People love to celebrate America's birthday on July 4th each year.

Happy Fourth of July!

Birthday parties are fun! The biggest birthday party in the United States is on July 4th every year. This party celebrates the birth of our nation.

At the beginning of 1776 our country was still ruled by the country of England. July 4, 1776 was a special day. It was the day our country decided to make its own rules and laws. People who make their own laws are independent. That is why July 4th is also Independence Day.

Towns and cities all over the United States celebrate our country's July 4th birthday. They all celebrate in different ways. Children and parents carry flags and balloons in parades.

They play baseball and go swimming. Some towns have watermelon eating contests. Families eat hamburgers and hot dogs cooked on outdoor grills.

People who live near lakes and rivers water-ski and have boat races. Cowboys in Montana and Wyoming ride bucking horses in rodeos. Cowgirls do trick riding. They stand up in the saddle, or they jump on and off the horse while it runs.

At night on July 4th, fireworks light up the sky. There are spinning red, white, and blue pinwheels. Rockets sparkle like stars. The air smells like gunpowder.

People who can't go to a park to see fireworks watch them on television. Every year there are special music and fireworks in Washington, D.C. Washington, D.C. is the capital of our country.

History of Independence Day

People in our country have fun celebrating July 4th today. But over 200 years ago in July 1776, our country's founders were not having fun. Many men and boys were fighting in a war called the American Revolution. The government was not like the one we have today. The country had only thirteen colonies instead of fifty states.

The thirteen colonies were all beside the Atlantic Ocean. Many colonists came from England, a country thousands of miles across the Atlantic Ocean. England's King George III ruled the colonies in America. He also ruled other parts of the world.

The king sent soldiers to America to make the colonists obey his laws. Some of these laws made the colonists pay high taxes. Other laws made them give food and shelter to the English soldiers.

Many colonists did not like what the king told them to do. In 1773 some colonists wanted to show that they did not like the tax on tea. One night about fifty colonists dressed up like Native Americans. They sneaked on board three British ships in Boston Harbor. Then they threw 300 chests of tea overboard! This event is called the Boston Tea Party.

Each one of the thirteen American colonies had its own leaders. These men helped their own colonies make laws. In 1774 they met in Philadelphia, Pennsylvania. This meeting was called the Continental Congress. The men talked about the ways England was being unfair to the colonies.

The next year the war began between the king's soldiers and the colonists. The English

Independence Hall is in Philadelphia, Pennsylvania. The Continental Congress first met in this building in 1774.

soldiers had guns, ships, and fancy uniforms. The colonists were not trained soldiers. They did not have uniforms. But they kept on fighting the English soldiers.

The colonists were not trained soldiers, but they fought hard against the English soldiers.

George Washington was a colonist from Virginia. He was a trained soldier. Later he became president of the United States. The Continental Congress asked him to lead the American soldiers. He said yes. The colonists won some battles. But the war went on.

The First Independence Day

The Continental Congress met again in 1775. They chose John Hancock of Virginia to be president of the Congress.

Another leader of the Congress was Richard Henry Lee. He said the colonists did not have to obey the king of England. John Adams, Benjamin Franklin, and Thomas Jefferson were some of the other leaders. They liked Lee's ideas.

The leaders talked together a lot. Sometimes they argued. On July 2, 1776, they finally decided what to tell King George. They all agreed that they wanted to govern themselves. They also wanted to make their own laws. They asked Thomas Jefferson to write down their ideas for a new government. They wanted to be one nation that had many colonies or states.

Jefferson read his paper to the other leaders. Some did not like all the new ideas. They were afraid that England would win the war. Then the king would be more strict. The colonists would be punished more.

Finally they all voted for a new government for the colonies. The new plan was called the Declaration of Independence. The first words were: "The unanimous declaration of the thirteen United States of America . . ." It said that the colonists would now choose their own leaders. And they would make their own laws.

The leaders agreed on the words for the Declaration on July 4th. That is why we celebrate on July 4th. But the leaders were not ready to tell the news to the people yet.

First they needed to make copies of the Declaration. They wanted to send a copy to each of the thirteen colonies. Jefferson gave his handwritten copy to a printer.

In CONGRESS. July 4. 1776.

The unanimous Declaration of the thirteen united States of America.

The Declaration of Independence was agreed to on July 4th, 1776.

On July 8 the printed copies of the Declaration were ready. Each leader got one. At last! The colonies could celebrate.

That day there was a big crowd outside the Philadelphia meeting hall at noontime. Chiefs of six Indian Nations joined the leaders of the Continental Congress.

A bell-ringer climbed up to the steeple. He quickly pulled the rope that rang the bell. Then a man stood on the front steps of the meeting hall. He read the Declaration of Independence to the crowd. Philadelphia church bells began to ring. The people cheered. Then they ran to tell others. They burned pictures of King George. They pulled down statues of him.

The Declaration gave all the people new hope. Now they believed that they could win the war against England. The colonists did win the war seven years later. It was 1783. Their country was free.

People have been celebrating Independence Day with colorful fireworks since 1777.

Celebrating on July 4th

John Adams worked hard helping to write the Declaration. He said that people would always celebrate July 4th because that was the day the Declaration was adopted. Adams' words turned out to be true. The colonies celebrated on that day every year afterward.

In 1777 people in Philadelphia put lighted candles in the windows of their homes. They also celebrated with bonfires and fireworks. Leaders of the new government gave speeches.

On July 4, 1788, Philadelphia had a big parade. There were many floats. The floats were decorated wagons pulled by horses. There was a giant-sized eagle on one float. The bald eagle is one symbol of the United States. This float was pulled by six white horses. A real ship, the *Union*, was on another float. The ship was thirty-four feet long.

Settlers who moved out west also celebrated July 4th. The first big celebration in Los Angeles, California, was on July 4, 1847. Soldiers cut down two trees. Then they fastened them together to make a tall flag pole. At sunrise on July 4 the soldiers marched to the top of a hill. They raised the American flag to the top of the new pole. Leaders read the Declaration of Independence in English and Spanish. There was a grand ball in the evening. A grand ball is a special dance where people dress up in fancy clothes.

More cities joined in celebrations or festivals every year. On July 4, 1848, people gathered in Washington, D.C. They placed the cornerstone for the Washington Monument. A cornerstone is set at the corner of a building or monument. The date and sometimes a little history are carved on the cornerstone. The Washington Monument is 555 feet tall and honors George Washington.

People in small villages celebrated too. Littlefork, Minnesota had a parade every year. They waved tiny flags. But the town wanted a big flag for July 4, 1921. Ladies in that town made a red, white, and blue quilt. They sewed the patches together in lines to look like stripes

The Washington Monument honors George Washington.

on the flag. The quilt decorated the Model-T Ford car that led the parade.

In 1941 many other countries were fighting a war. Our leaders knew the United States might go to war too. That year they made July 4 a holiday for everyone in the United States.

The Centennial and Bicentennial Celebrations

A century is 100 years. A centennial celebrates the 100th anniversary of an event. Our country's centennial was on July 4, 1876.

People across the United States celebrated 100 years of independence. The biggest celebration was in Philadelphia. The city invited every country in the world to a special celebration. This event was called the International Exposition.

Visitors saw many exciting exhibits at the Exposition. One exhibit had only things made by women. Another one showed Alexander Graham Bell's telephone and Thomas Edison's telegraph. There was the first railroad car that kept foods cold. Another exhibit showed new uses for electricity. People saw electricity ring bells and burglar alarms. It also operated traffic signals.

People saw a famous painting called "The Spirit of '76" for the first time. Archibald Willard of Bedford, Ohio, was the artist. The painting shows a scene on the battlefield during the American Revolution. Willard's father was the model for the tall drummer in the center. Willard's soldier friend posed as the fife player. Henry Devereux posed for the drummer boy.

The painting was shown in many cities across the country after the Exposition. Today it is in Abbott Hall in the city of Marblehead, Massachusetts.

The people in Los Angeles, California celebrated the centennial with a long parade. Marchers were soldiers, city people, and ranchers. Buildings were decorated with green vines and colored streamers. Pretty girls rode on floats pulled by horses. They wore banners that

The painting "The Spirit of '76" was displayed for the first time across the United States during the centennial in 1876.

said "Miss Liberty," "Miss Peace," and "Miss Plenty." More than 1500 people heard band music and sang songs. A city leader read the Declaration of Independence. Everyone ate lots of food. Then they watched fireworks in the evening.

Two centuries is 200 years. A 200th anniversary is called a bicentennial. July 4, 1976, was the 200th anniversary of the beginning of our country's independence.

Towns and cities all over the country planned special events. In Philadelphia they cleaned and decorated Independence Hall.

In Washington, D.C. people dressed in the kinds of clothes people wore in 1776. Children helped make candles. They dipped long strings called wicks into wax. Women cooked food in open fireplaces. They made soap in big tubs.

Blacksmiths pounded hot metal into horseshoes and many kinds of tools. These activities showed how different life was 200 years ago.

These third grade children dressed in the kinds of clothes people wore in 1776. They learned what life was like during colonial times.

In Boston, people dressed up to look like colonists during the American Revolution. A man rode a horse along the same route Paul Revere took in 1775. In that year Revere galloped through the streets to warn the colonists about the British soldiers. He shouted, "The British are coming! The British are coming!"

The American Freedom Train started traveling across the country from east to west. It carried George Washington's copy of the Declaration of Independence. Copies of famous pictures and other papers were on this train. It stopped in eighty cities across the United States. People got on the train to look at the displays.

People in Boston heard a symphony orchestra play "The 1812 Overture." This music was composed by Peter Tchaikovsky. Real cannons boomed in time with the music. Church bells rang. Fireworks shot high into the sky.

In New York, 212 tall sailing ships from thirty-four countries gathered in the harbor.

These were the largest sailing ships in the world. One of the American ships was the U.S.S. *Eagle*. It is the cadet training ship for the United States Coast Guard. A giant-size national flag hung from a bridge over the Hudson River. The tall ships sailed under this flag. More than six million people saw the ships and the flag.

Lots of towns across the country have parades on Independence Day.

July 4th Today

Every July 4th there's a neighborhood parade for children and parents in Durham, North Carolina. Some children pull their pets in wagons. One boy carried his pet ducks. A girl tied red, white, and blue ribbons on her dog.

Many children make their own costumes to wear in the parade. Parents march too. Some push babies in strollers. After the parade, everybody sings "My Country 'Tis of Thee." Then they recite the Pledge of Allegiance. The first Durham parade was more than 40 years ago. There were only six children in it. Now more than 150 children and parents march each year.

The first parade in Bristol, Rhode Island, was

in 1865. That's more than 125 years ago. In 1992 it had forty floats, twenty-nine bands, and thousands of marchers.

On July 4 in Ojai, California, the Lions Club has a pancake breakfast. Campfire girls sell lemonade. Boy Scouts and Girl Scouts serve a spaghetti dinner. Some families have picnics on park lawns. They listen to the County Symphony Orchestra play a concert. At night, everyone goes to the school grounds and watches fireworks.

Shenandoah, Iowa, celebrates July 4th with many events. Children have a pet show. An airplane flies overhead. It tows a banner that says "God Bless America."

There is a dunk tank in the park. The school principal sits on a board over a big tub of water. People rent three baseballs for twenty-five cents. Each person tries to hit a target with the ball. If the ball hits the target, the principal falls into the water.

Many towns have parades. Some have

A favorite game on July 4th is the dunk tank. The player tries to hit a target with a baseball. If he does, the person sitting on the board above the tank falls in.

marching bands, clowns, and floats. People on the sidewalks wave flags, laugh, and clap.

Members of the Shriner's Club drive tiny cars in parades. The men in this club give money to help children. The Shriners wear special hats called fezzes. The hats look like upside-down flower pots with tassels.

In some parades, Shriners wearing fezzes and waving flags circle and weave along the street in little "funny cars."

In Bridgeport, California, children have watermelon-eating contests on July 4th. The one who eats the most slices wins. Some towns have watermelon-seed-spitting contests. The winner is the one who spits a seed that farthest.

In Albany, Oregon, the July 4th celebration is a world-championship timber carnival. Some men chop logs in a contest. The winner is the one who chops through a large log first.

Tree-climbing is another contest at the timber carnival. Men and women wear sharp spikes on their boots. Each ties a rope around his or her waist and around the trees. These ropes help them climb. The one who climbs to the top and back down first is the winner.

The Horribles Parade is held every July 4th in Marblehead, Massachusetts. Everybody wears a funny costume. One boy wore a lobster fisherman's oilskin coat and hat. He pulled a lobster trap in his red wagon.

The town of Independence, California, was named for Fort Independence. The fort was first used on July 4, 1862. It protected settlers against the Native Americans. The town celebrates with a parade every July 4th. Children decorate their tricycles and bicycles for the parade. Afterward they have different kinds of races in the park. Some children bring frogs for a frog-jumping contest.

Famous Symbols of Independence

Thousands of visitors go to Washington, D.C., Philadelphia, and New York each year. Many go to see the symbols of our nation's independence.

The Declaration of Independence. The original copy of the Declaration of Independence is in the National Archives building in Washington, D.C. Visitors can read the words that Thomas Jefferson wrote. The Continental Congress finally approved the Declaration on August 2, 1776. This copy has the signatures of the fifty-six members of the Continental Congress who signed the Declaration on that day.

The U.S. Flag. Nobody really knows who made the first flag. On June 14, 1777, the Continental Congress described the flag it wanted. There were thirteen red and white stripes. These represented the first thirteen colonies. Then thirteen white stars were put on a blue background in one corner. Today there are fifty stars. They represent the fifty states in the nation. The flag stands for the government, the land, and the people of the United States. People all over the world know that the American flag is a symbol of freedom.

June 14 each year is honored as the birthday of the flag. The largest flag ever made was flown on Flag Day in 1992. It was on a farm near Philadelphia. It was 500 feet long and 260 feet wide. Each stripe was over twenty feet wide. Each star was sixteen feet across.

The American flag has different names. It is called "The Stars and Stripes" most often. William Driver was a sea captain from Salem, Massachusetts. He called the flag "Old Glory."

The American flag is a symbol of freedom in our country. These girls are getting ready to carry the flag in an Independence Day parade.

Francis Scott Key called the flag "The Star Spangled Banner." In 1814 the Americans and the British were fighting again. When the Americans saved Fort McHenry, Key wrote a poem about it. Later an actor sang those words to the tune of an old song. In March 1931 Congress voted to make the song our country's national anthem.

The Liberty Bell. The Liberty Bell was made in England in 1752. It weighs more than 2,000 pounds. The bell cracked when it was being rung in 1753. It broke again in 1835. It was fixed both times. It is now protected in a park near Independence Hall in Philadelphia.

Independence Hall. Independence Hall is the most famous building in Philadelphia. Its first name was the Old State House. The leaders of the thirteen colonies met here in 1774 and 1775. This is where they planned to unite against England. They chose George Washington as the Commander in Chief of the Army.

On July 4, 1776, the Declaration of

The Liberty Bell is in Philadelphia. It is protected in a special park near Independence Hall.

Independence was adopted here. On July 8, the Liberty Bell rang from the Hall's bell tower. This was to celebrate the new declaration.

The Statue of Liberty. The Statue of Liberty is one of the largest statues ever made. It stands on Liberty Island at the entrance to New York Harbor. People on every ship that sails into the harbor see it.

Some people call the statue "Miss Liberty." It is a symbol of freedom for all. It was a gift to the United States from the country of France. It was presented to America on July 4, 1884. Frederic Auguste Bartholdi designed it.

Visitors climb 189 steps inside the statue to the top of the pedestal. Then they climb 154 more steps up to the crown. From there they look down on the harbor and New York City.

The Great Seal. The Great Seal is on all important papers of the United States. It was adopted in 1782, six years after the Declaration of Independence. John Adams, Thomas Jefferson, and Benjamin Franklin designed it.

The Statue of Liberty is one of the largest statues ever made. Some people call the statue "Miss Liberty."

The American bald eagle is on the front of the seal. The eagle's head is covered in white feathers. That makes it look bald. This bird was chosen as a symbol because it is large and powerful. It holds an olive branch in one of its talons. Talon is another name for a bird's claw. The olive branch stands for peace. The branch has thirteen leaves and thirteen olives. These represent the thirteen original colonies. The eagle holds thirteen arrows in the other talon. The arrows stands for war. The olive branch shows that America wants peace. The arrows mean that it will fight when it has to.

The eagle holds a rolled-up paper in its beak. This paper is also called a scroll. There are Latin words written on it. They mean "one out of many." This means that one nation was created out of many states.

The first Independence Day was more than 200 years ago. Other countries are older. But ours is famous for its many freedoms. One of these freedoms is the right to choose our own leaders. Another freedom lets us speak and write what we think.

Each year thousands of people come to the United States from other countries. They come to enjoy freedom in our country. They help us celebrate the birthday of freedom in the United States on July 4th.

In the United States, the "Spirit of '76" lives on.

Glossary

blacksmith—A person who makes horseshoes, tools, and other things out of metal.

bonfire—A large outdoor fire.

cadet—A student training to be an officer in the army, navy, air force, or coast guard.

colonist—One of the people who lives in a colony. The first American settlers were colonists.

cornerstone—A stone at the corner of a new building or monument, often laid at a ceremony when the building is first begun.

exposition—A large show or event that is open to the public.

fez—A felt hat that is usually red. It looks like an upside-down flower pot, with a long, black tassel.

fife—A musical instrument that looks like a small flute.

float—A low, flat vehicle used to carry displays and people in a parade.

founder—A person who brings an idea, event, or a place into being.

grand ball—A large party where guests wear fancy clothes and dance together.

independence—Freedom from the influence or control of other people or countries.

Model-T Ford—A car built by Henry Ford in 1908.

monument—A building or other structure that honors the memory of a famous person or event.

patriotic—Showing great love for one's country and loyalty to it.

pinwheel—A small firework that spins and throws off colored sparks.

rocket—A firework that leaves a trail of colored sparks when it shoots into the sky.

steeple—A tower rising above the main part of a building. Many churches have steeples.

symbol—A thing that stands for a person, place or idea.

symphony orchestra—A large orchestra that has many different kinds of instruments.

unanimous—Showing complete agreement.

Index